# Agile Ceremonies :

# The details you were missing

Dmitri Iarandine

# Contents

# Introduction

Welcome to the third book in the series of publications written to help the Agile practitioners get better at what they do, progressing their careers through the busy job markets of Digital Delivery, Agile Project Management roles, and beyond.

I've started writing about how a skilled and motivated professional could pivot their career towards the market of "Agile jobs", setting the goal of becoming a Scrum Master. Then I've released another book aimed to help the existing Scrum Masters broaden their skillset and learn about Agile Coaching as a potential further career move.

This book will go back to basics and teach you all the ins and outs of the key Agile events and ceremonies that any good Scrum Master, Product Owner, Agile Business Analyst or Project Manager should be familiar with.

While the Scrum Guide tells you what each Scrum ceremony is about, I've seen numerous freshly appointed Scrum Masters who had literally no idea how to run any of those.

The only exception was unsurprisingly the famous "Daily Stand-up" that everyone appears to be doing these days. It's the ceremony that's the hardest to do wrong too, due to its simplicity and clarity of purpose. But even in this case, I've witnessed many examples of poor practices and lingering confusion among all of the participants.

I hope this book is going to bridge this knowledge gap for a lot of you.

By the end of the last chapter, you should have a very good understanding of the context and all steps involved in running any of the key Agile Scrum ceremonies. I'll also offer you a few additional team-building and broader purpose activities that a good Agile team should strive to do once in a while.

The Conclusion chapter will suggest some directions of your further professional growth, should you choose to continue your journey of becoming an all-rounded Lean-Agile practitioner.

If you can't wait to jump into the depths of the process involved in all of the Agile ceremonies this book has to offer you, feel free to proceed to the next chapter and dive right in.

If you'd appreciate a little extra context and frame of thought that I had when planning out the content of this book, I'd like to offer you the rest of this chapter, starting with this very familiar line from the Agile Manifesto:

**Individuals and Interactions** *over* **Processes and Tools**

The founders of the Agile movement made an effort to highlight that Processes and Tools remained important to us in many ways, while the lacking Interactions and collaboration with Individuals deserved some extra attention back in 2001 when the Agile Manifesto was first published.

As time went on and we've embraced the Agile values and practiced Agile methods in many real-life scenarios, it became evident that Processes and Tools stretched over a broad range of activities, practices and enabling solutions that kept their dominant presence in the minds of those attempting an Agile transformation in their organization.

Processes and Tools are the most visible layer of the well-known "Agile Onion" diagram, while Values, Principles and the Mindset remain hidden from sight, sometimes for many months or even years. This effect detracts from their perceived importance to the company investing the efforts in becoming more Agile.

Even almost twenty years after the Agile Manifesto got published and many teams started practicing Agile all over the World, those changed processes and tools that visualize teamwork or increase collaboration have been at the forefront of any Agile Transformation that I've witnessed.

Some coaching and change management models even suggest reliance on the rigid and clear definition of freshly introduced structures, such as the new Agile roles, clear responsibilities, and ceremonies to drive the whole Agile Transformation forward.

You could consider yourself being a purist Agile practitioner who would put more effort into the slow-paced but solid introduction of Agile values and principles for the team to live by, or feel like someone who would put the new Agile ceremonies forward as one of the Tools that will help build Agile culture over time.

Regardless of your approach and personal preferences as an Agile influencer and practitioner, having a richer set of Tools and Processes that you could use when the situation calls for it would make your professional life much easier.

What I'm getting at here is that the Processes are still important!

And the Agile ceremonies that help build the Agile culture driving any Agile Transformation forward need to remain meaningful and be done the right way to bring value to the participating team.

Why is it so hard to get the basic Agile processes - ceremonies and events - right from the start?

Mainly because the Agile facilitators and champions of the transformation movement "learn on the job". Very few people get an opportunity to witness a correctly conducted Agile ceremony before they literally hit the ground running and start shadowing an existing Scrum Master, Iteration Manager, or an Agile Coach - if they are lucky.

We get thrown into the deep end of the boiling Agile pot as new practitioners and pick up some basic practices and rituals as we go, rarely investing time into learning how to run or execute those practices properly.

Having a dedicated Agile Coach on the ground certainly helps in that more natural and environment-specific learning process, but another hard truth is that not many Agile Delivery professionals have that luxury.

While Agile Coach is a common and well-recognized role in Agile Transformations landscape, not every layer of the organization has one available to the necessary extent, where they could properly show you the tricks of the trade such as how to run your Agile ceremonies better, beyond a couple of Sprint Planning sessions and Retrospectives.

I really hope that this worst-case scenario of a hypothetical situation where you have no other source that could give you a sufficient amount of detail to get started with those Agile ceremonies can be resolved with the help of this book!

# Who is this book for?

This book was written mainly for the Agile Digital Product Delivery and Project Management professionals, who are expected to facilitate any of the Agile ceremonies and events as part of their participation in an Agile Transformation of some kind.

The list of potential roles could include but wouldn't be limited to:

- Scrum Masters
- Iteration Managers
- Agile Delivery Managers
- Agile Product Owners
- Agile Business Analysts
- Agile Coaches
- Agile Project Managers (to a lesser extent)

# Prerequisites

If you've read any of my other books you'd know that I like to ramble a little bit, trying to give my reader as much of the relevant context and my related thoughts wherever possible. Guilty as charged!

This time I'm making a conscious effort to keep the extra detail to a minimum and focus on providing a rich description of each Agile ceremony we'll be looking into. After a brief context that is largely unavoidable if you're trying to make sure your reader isn't caught off-guard with specific details, I'll offer you steps that you should follow to facilitate the event.

Planning the content of the book this way means there are some expectations or prerequisites, meeting which would make sure you're not missing anything important.

Those prerequisites include:

## Your knowledge of the Agile Manifesto

Make sure you've read it, understood all the key values, and checked out the twelve core principles of Agile value delivery;

## Your knowledge of the Scrum Guide

Scrum Guide is a freely available resource that serves as the baseline for too many things across the Agile domain, and all of the ceremonies we'll be discussing in this book are outlined at a high-level in the Scrum Guide. There is absolutely no excuse for you to not read the Scrum Guide a couple of times and make sure you understand the core concepts before trying to learn the detailed process that I'll offer you.

I'll make a lot of references to the Scrum Guide, so the better versed in it you are, the more value you'll get from reading the following chapters, feeling more in control of your professional actions as a Scrum Master, Agile Product Owner, or playing any other role in an Agile Transformation where you'd have to facilitate or guide your Team through those ceremonies.

The amount of extra context I'll offer you before explaining how to play a certain Agile Game with your team, or how to run a certain Agile ceremony will depend on how common I believe that game or ceremony is.

For example, when explaining how to properly run a Sprint Planning session, I won't offer you as much introductory context as I'd do for a Backlog Refinement session, which is just as important, but a lot less formal and having too many ways to approach it. Any ambiguity of the process calls for extra detail, and I'm not going to shy away from offering it to you, because I believe this is exactly what you've been missing so far, and the main reason for you to pick up this book.

# How is this book structured?

Each chapter of this book describes how to run one particular Agile ceremony or activity, telling you everything you really need to know to prepare and achieve the desired outcomes.

The only exception will be the chapter talking about Agile Energizers and "Ice-Breaker" exercises, as I was able to fit a number of those into one chapter. Knowing a number of those team-building and warm-up activities is what often differentiates a green Scrum Master from an aspiring or even more experienced Agile Coach.

None of the chapters describing activities and ceremonies explicitly mention the points that apply across the board, and could be considered obvious. Including:

## 1. Making sure the right people are in the room

Descriptions of most ceremonies will offer you my suggestions of who should be in attendance and sometimes what roles those people should play, but the fact that you need to identify and include those "right" people in the meeting will be assumed as obvious.

## 2. Providing enough context for the team

This mainly means making sure everyone understands - at least at high-level - what's about to happen and why.

This element should be easy if you are facilitating Agile ceremonies for an existing team that perhaps had the appropriate Agile or Scrum training, but will require a more conscious effort from you at the start of any ceremony - if they did not have any prior introductions.

In the context of Agile Energisers, Ice-Breakers and warm-up games, you should almost always briefly explain the purpose and high-level outline of the activity that you're proposing for everyone to engage in. This would help ensure more active and willing participation from the team members, or perhaps someone would choose to opt-out and not participate - which should be always left to the choice of an individual.

Never force people to do anything, including playing your Agile games!

With this introduction out of the way, let's get started and jump straight into Chapter 1, that will tell you about the process of Backlog creation and refinement.

# Chapter 1 – Backlog Refinement

One of the major contributing factors to the successful Digital Product delivery is ensuring that the whole team has visibility and access to the well-refined Product Backlog.

Old-school agilists like yours truly remember the good-old-days when we used a simpler term of "*Backlog grooming*". The term then went out of fashion, due to the growing societal sensitivity to the meaning associated with a whole range of words. I thought I'll mention this old - and still occasionally used - term here for completeness of this little guide though.

Backlog refinement is a process that a Product Owner goes through to make sure their Product Backlog Items (PBIs) actually mean something to the Developers who will be asked to estimate and do the work.

Many elements of the refinement process are very similar or directly related to the Backlog creation - where you add new work items to the initially empty Backlog bucket in your Team collaboration tool. So I thought I'd focus on refinement as a more continuous and involved process, letting you use your professional skills and common sense to apply the same technique to create the initial set of work items, before refining them.

The process itself is seen as a continuous effort that doesn't have a strictly prescribed form or procedure associated with it, so we'll focus on the expected outcomes of this process instead. What does the Product Owner need to achieve to ensure that the rest of their Scrum Team could actually get started and deliver value at the end of the Sprint?

Looking at Backlog Refinement as a recurring session where the Product Owner works with the Developers to break down work and add detail to the PBIs, I'd suggest that you tried to achieve the following outcomes:

1. Make sure the PBIs are worded clearly enough to convey how does a specific type of End-user benefit from the value from completing those work Items;

2. Make sure the PBIs include clear conditions of satisfaction or the Acceptance Criteria. Developers need to know when will the Product Owner formally sees any particular item "Done", and the Testers need to understand what conditions they'd need to test for, to ensure that the item has no defects in it.

In a nutshell, it's that simple and comes down to these two high-level points.

Everything else we do as part of Backlog Refinement is really cheating the classic Scrum Framework or any other development process, trying to save time in the future by pre-empting certain activities, such as PBI estimation, before the actual Sprint Planning had a chance to take place.

So we'll keep things simple in this chapter and now focus on the following suggested steps involved in Backlog Refinement process:

# Step 1 – Present the Backlog Item

Product Owner presents a Backlog Item that they'd like to refine or break down further.

They tell the development team what they know about the End-user needs supporting the creation of this item, usually also briefly explaining why they see this item as valuable and obviously heading the team's way over the next Sprint or two.

The developers would ask questions to better understand the amount of work required to complete the item or even just familiarise themselves with an area of domain knowledge or Business process that they've never encountered before.

Your mileage will vary here dramatically, as the duration and format of this step will heavily depend on how much do the developers know about the type of work, technical systems, processes and any other requirements that would be involved in the completion of this task.

# Step 2 (*Optional*) – Preliminary Work Breakdown

This is where you'll decompose the Work Item into smaller pieces, if the Product Owner and the development team agree that it's the best way forward.

After some discussion that could be quite lengthy sometimes, the whole team might agree to break the presented Item into multiple ones, if it appears to be too big of an effort. This split of the Item is also recommended when the developers simply "don't know" even how to approach this particular technical functionality and need to perform what is best known as a "Technical Spike", before committing to completion of that particular presented PBI.

We'll talk about the Technical Spike in the section below, but the situation where the team feels like the proposed Backlog Item is too large to fit into one Sprint, needing to be split in two or more separate User Stories appears more straightforward.

If a Backlog Item needing refinement read as:

"*As a User, I need to have access to a shopping cart so I can order items online.*"

It would appear to me that unless the team dealt with a simple Shopping Portal configuration requirement, where the shopping cart could be enabled relatively easily, this User Story would require extensive development and testing effort.

In this case, I'd imagine the team discussing the key elements or functions that would power the shopping cart, what would constitute its most basic form, and which features would be added extras, and then splitting the User story accordingly.

There is also a way of looking at this example as "promoting" the original Backlog Item to the level of a Feature or an Epic - depending on what work decomposition hierarchy the Product Owner proposed to the team and their Business stakeholders - and creating the new set of User Stories under it, as a child-parent relationship.

We could end up with the following split Stories or children of a shopping cart creation Feature:

*"As a User, I need a page on the Portal where I can see my planned purchases...."*
*"As a User, I need to be able to mark advertised items as intended to be purchased..."*
*"As a User, I need to be able to remove the marked items from my shopping list..."*
*"As a User, I need to be able to provide my postal address..."*

and so on.

Are these the most purist User Stories that are expressing only the Customer's goal and not hinting at the proposed solution at all? Possibly not.

But this is the taste of reality of what many of the Product Owners and Scrum Masters have to deal with and accept as "good enough" in the vast majority of cases you'll realistically encounter.

# Step 3 (*Optional*) – Agreeing to do a Technical Spike

This is where the team might decide that the amount of information is insufficient to commit to starting the work on a particular User Story or Task, and that further technical capability or systems availability investigation is required.

Let's use an example of a User Story that originally read as:

*"As a User I want to be instantly notified about any changes to my account via SMS so that I could learn about the latest events while on the go."*

The developers might see the value that the Story brings to the User and why the Product Owner sees it as important, but could immediately tell that it suggests reliance on an SMS gateway that they aren't sure is operational yet.

So instead of working through the detailed Acceptance Criteria with the Product Owner they strongly suggest conducting a time-boxed Technical Spike Task that would aim to ensure availability and basic functionality of the proprietary SMS gateway their company uses for security reasons.

The Product Owner would hopefully agree to this sensible proposal that comes from the technical and systems knowledge of their development team and create a new Technical Spike Task in the Product Backlog, stating the need to determine connectivity with SMS gateway and a few other high-level requirements.

I hope this slightly crude example made sense to you too. The idea is to collaborate pre-emptively, where possible, and achieve the following benefits:

1. Provide visibility of the new work that's going to reach the development team over the next couple of weeks;

2. Give them a chance to negotiate with the Product Owner pre-emptively, achieving early alignment on the direction and features they'd be slating for the further upcoming Sprints;

3. Cut a few more corners where possible, perhaps getting a high-level and early estimate from the Team for a few Backlog Items,

and therefore having a much quicker and easier time to re-estimate the Item at the next Sprint Planning.

# Backlog Refinement as a background activity

As mentioned already, the actual process of continuous Backlog refinement in the background is largely up to the Product Owner, as long as they keep their main goals in mind. They need to obtain as much information about Customer needs that are applicable to their Product or Service they are building and maintaining, translating that information into an overarching Vision and the Feature Roadmap.

When the Vision for the Product is clear, the Product Owner should be able to come up with a few prominent milestones that would enable progressive releases of that Customer Value in the form of a Minimal Viable Product (MVP), and the following feature releases 1, 2, 3 or however many the Product Owner can foresee.

Needless to say that both the Product Vision and the Roadmap guiding further work breakdown and Backlog refinement are evolving artifacts, not set in stone and forgotten from the moment of the Project work kicking off.

While seeming not directly connected to the process of a Backlog refinement, having that Vision for the Product and a progressively evolving prioritized pipeline of features in the form of a roadmap would serve as a compass and the Northern Star for the Product Owner to make the best work decomposition and prioritization decisions.

As the Scrum Master or a Coach assisting the Product Owner with getting into the groove of that continuous Backlog refinement process, you'd encourage them to start with larger functional pieces and then seeing the valuable moving parts inside those pieces, which would serve as your primary candidates for work decomposition.

Specific refinement of the Backlog is always up to the Product Owner and a group of Subject-Matter Experts (SMEs) assisting them with technical insight when it comes to a sensible breakdown of larger pieces of work into smaller ones - as we've discussed in the section above.

As far as Product Owner-driven work decomposition and refinement are concerned though, I'd recommend starting by recognizing the following six work breakdown options:

# 1. By functions or distinct Product workflow steps

For example, if the Feature or a high-level User Story talk about notifying the User about certain changes to their account, the process of work breakdown and further refinement could involve capturing of separate steps or notification features supported by the platform that the Product is being built upon.

Split User Stories along the following lines would come to mind here:

*"As a User, I want to see the key notifications on my Portal dashboard so that I immediately see what requires my attention"*

*"As a User, I want to receive a notification via the text message on my mobile phone so that I can be informed of any important updates while on the go"*

*"As a User, I want to receive a notification email so that I can stay informed about the latest updates even without direct access to the Portal or my mobile phone"*

These examples of various types of notifications could be seen as individual functions that the Product Owner can prioritize appropriately, or they might be the steps of one notification workflow, that ideally would do all three things in a certain order.

## 2. By specific Business Rules

What's the difference between Business Rules and specific functions that we've briefly looked at above? It's usually in the nuances of how your particular organization defines the two. The line differentiating the two could be hard to spot, yet in some organizations or digital product engineering environments it would be very clear.

Looking at another example would be probably the easiest way to demonstrate this:

If the Feature or a high-level User Story requiring further refinement and breakdown would read as:

*"As a logged-in User, I want to see only the information I really need so that I don't have to waste time scrolling through the list of various notifications trying to find the right entry"*

Admittedly, I've seen better User Stories, but I guess it conveys what the User is after while not suggesting a specific solution of how they'd want to trim down the amount of information that the notifications area of their Online Portal would offer them in an unfiltered way.

So the User Stories that the Product Owner could pencil in for further refinement with the Team could read as:

*"As a User, I want to be able to sort the notification list entries by date so that I can find what I need easier"*

*"As a User, I want to have access to a free text keyword search so that I can find exactly what I need among all the list entries"*

*"As a User, I want to have a pre-set list of filters that I could quickly choose from to trim down the amount of information offered to me"*

# 3. By variations in data

Variations in data could be vastly different, yet offering clear delineation between development pieces of work.

One of the relatively clear examples of User Story refinement and breakdown here could be enabling certain features or User Interface elements in different languages:

*"As an International Student, I want to be able to navigate the Portal efficiently so that I could easily find the courses that I'm interested to apply for"*

Could be broken down into:

*"As an International Student, I want to see the navigation of the Portal presented to me in Arabic"*

Naturally, you'd add more languages and consider refining the work items further if it seems sensible to isolate the effort to update main navigation from some other prominent UI elements of the portal.

Remember the rule of thumb - no invisible work!

## 4. By important system qualities

Sometimes you knew that the platform and systems that your specific digital Product or Service are being built upon have limitations or specific dependencies that provide opportunities to refine work items further.

For example, if your team is building features into a Smart Home management solution, there could be a high-level User Story stating:

*"As a Smart Home Customer I want to have access to the most accurate energy consumption data so that I feel in control of my energy spend in the given month"*

Knowing the qualities of the system enabling the process of reading the data from the Customer's premises, the Product Owner could refine this User Story or split it into the more technical and specific Features or Tasks:

*"... enable data interpolation from the last known energy meter reading ... "*

or

*"... visualize real-time data pulled on-demand directly from the energy meter ...".*

# 5. By specific User Types or Personas

An absolutely best-known favourite among more experienced Product Owners or Agile Business Analysts who deal with Backlog refinement and various forms of work decomposition into User Stories this recommendation revolves around defining Agile Personas or applicable User Groups.

Starting your Agile Delivery process with a Discovery Session where you define specific User Journeys and Personas that serve as a virtual name and grouping of those User groups, is of paramount importance here.

That could offer work decomposition along the following lines:

*"As a Portal User, I want..."*

could become a lot more specific and useful to the Developers for planning their work, and the Business stakeholders for prioritizing the importance of those features and accepting the work as done:

*"As a Teacher, I want... "*
*"As a Portal Administrator, I want..."*

*"As an Online Course Coordinator, I want..."*

## 6. By specific Customer Segments

Very similar to the User Types and Personas, Customer Segments could be something that would appear more obvious to the Product Owner given the nature of their Product or Service at the time of Backlog refinement.

A User Story starting as:

*"As a Customer, I want...."*

would then become more specific and prioritization-friendly:

*"As a Small Business Customer, I want..."*
*"As a Wholesale Customer, I want..."*
*"As a Retail Customer, I want...."*

Hopefully the information provided in this chapter gives you a good idea of the two types of Backlog Refinement processes - as a background activity for the Product Owner to do continuously as the new information emerges from the Customers and Business stakeholders of the organization, and as a recurring meeting with the development team where the high-level User Stories and proposed Tasks could be detailed and negotiated further, with the insight from the technical experts of the team.

It is up to your personal preference, specific role and the culture of your organization to determine which method of Refinement would work best.

Very commonly the Product Owners use both the background population and light-touch refinement of the Backlog on their own, leaving the bulky additions and coordination with the Development team to those specifically arranged meetings.

# Chapter 2 – Sprint Planning

Sprint Planning is one of the better-known and most important ceremonies coming to us from the Scrum Framework. While any Agile practitioner worth their money would immediately correct me here, saying that all of the Scrum ceremonies are important and were introduced for a good reason, some are skipped less frequently than others!

Keeping it real, as I try and do in all my books, I have to say that sometimes the bad practices such as bastardizing Scrum and skipping some ceremonies actually highlights what's perceived as adding the most and the least value for the Customer and the Scrum Team itself.

Using this environmental awareness as an Agile Coach, for example, could give you a lot of valuable information helping create your coaching plans, and generally determine the condition your transforming delivery environment is in.

Sprint Planning is a classic example of an unavoidable and all-important Agile ceremony that we'll take a very close look at in this chapter.

Key goals of any Sprint Planning are to discuss what the Product Owner would like done over the next Sprint, commit to what appears achievable, confirm the Sprint Goal, and formally start the Sprint as a Team.

The timing of the ceremony varies based on how long the Sprint is. Scrum Guide explains this part rather well, recommending to spend up to 8 hours planning the 4-week Sprint. Realistically, you'd probably never run into this situation.

With some exceptions, if you're looking at the body of work that is being delivered using Scrum Framework while requiring the full 4 weeks to create a demonstrable and valuable Product Increment, chances are that this work could be broken down much better.

This could also require some extra attention to the Scrum Team composition, but we are not going to deviate too much from the main topic of this chapter. The key to keeping your Team focused and efficient during Sprint Planning is preparation.

Certain activities that precede the Sprint Planning, such as the Backlog Refinement session that we've discussed in the previous chapter, are usually reducing the amount of complexity, the number of unknowns and therefore the required duration of the Sprint Planning itself.

Before we go through the exact steps involved in running a good Sprint Planning session, I'll briefly mention some anti-patterns that I've observed and would like you to be aware of. Those usually stem from the level of professional maturity of the facilitator, or the overall willingness of the Team to follow the proper process.

For example:

A classroom-trained Scrum Master facilitating a Sprint Planning might religiously stick to the key points from the Scrum Guide, making their Team jump through the formal hoops they never really needed. While another Scrum Master who never had any proper training or motivation and time to invest in their additional Agile education would likely skip some of the essential elements such as setting a Sprint Goal.

Regardless of what's happening out there in the Agile Wild West that is far too common behind many closed corporate doors, here we'll go through what I consider an efficient Sprint Planning meeting - given your preparation for the session.

# How to prepare

Make sure you've helped your Product Owner with the facilitation of a Backlog Refinement session that the whole Development Team participated in.

Book a room that comfortably fits the whole team, and won't feel too small or lacking air if you have to spend a couple of hours in there. Do not attempt Sprint Planning in open spaces - *as tempting as that might be* - until you know your team very well, and the process is happening almost automatically, with everyone knowing their roles, the body of work being reviewed and similar factors.

If your Scrum Team is not fully cross-functional and consists of the specialists whose capacity would have to be determined individually during the session, a whiteboard with some markers would help you visualize the process for everyone a little better.

I strongly recommend having a large screen or a projector that could be used to display the Product and Sprint Backlog for everyone to see and easily comment on.

# The process

There are several ways to run a good Sprint Planning in my view, but I'll give you only two variations that would work well following the process of Backlog Refinement that we've already looked at in this book.

The two variants I'll offer you here are the Sprint Planning Including Team Capacity and an easier one without any capacity calculations. Both processes flow quite similarly, but the easier one doesn't require a few extra optional steps that I'll clearly outline for you.

## Step 1 - Review the incomplete items of the current Sprint

Some highly efficient Scrum Teams that manage to plan their work conservatively, not over-commit, and complete all of the Backlog Items by the time the Sprint Review of the current Sprint happens would naturally skip this step.

The majority of real-life Scrum Teams that I've observed choose to reconcile and properly close off the Sprint as the first item on their Sprint Planning agenda.

You as the facilitator would encourage the Product Owner and Developers to take a quick look at each item on the team's Scrum Board and confirm those as "Not started", "Started, but incomplete", or even "Started, but obsolete, so discarded".

This is usually fluid and unstructured discussion that you should encourage as the facilitator, keeping the track of time and not letting the team go deep into over-analysing a particular item at this stage.

Ultimately, any unfinished items will return to the Product Backlog for reprioritization and possible acceptance into the next Sprint. A very common mistake I see among fresh Agile practitioners is the assumption that any unfinished item gets automatically allocated and accepted into the next Sprint.

This is not the case. Everything is subject to renegotiation.

## Step 2 - Close the current Sprint

After the quick discussion surrounding any unfinished or discarded items, the current Sprint is usually formally closed and the whole team looks at the high-level stats and numbers as the snapshot of their performance.

Depending on the collaboration tool or method your Scrum Team uses to visualize and track the work, one would expect to be able to see clear numbers of how many Stories and Tasks were completed, versus the overall number of those planned.

Burn-down chart and velocity tracking should be something on your radar as well, as long as the Team has been estimating the relative size of work items they've been delivering to date.

How many Story Points worth of work did the team complete?

## Step 3 (*Optional*) – Calculate the capacity of your team

Some teams simply review the list of Backlog Items that the Product Owner nominated as the most valuable and highest priority to be addressed during the next Sprint, and then use their subjective judgment and perhaps prior experience to determine how many of those items they'd be able to complete.

This optional step addresses a very common situation where:

1.  The prior historically-proven velocity of the Team isn't known, so committing to any volume of work over the next Sprint without calculating the actual capacity of the Development team would be nothing more than a guess;
2.  The Team isn't cross-functional and its capacity can't be treated as one large "bucket" to put the Sprint Backlog into. Individual developers would deal with specialization-based duties and therefore need to clearly indicate and commit to their available capacity to do this type of work over the upcoming Sprint.

I'd suggest to keep it simple until you've gotten to know the team better and perhaps determined a more optimal way that suits you and the team better than the process described below.

Create a table or a matrix of names of your team members who will be doing the work - Developers and Testers - clearly indicating their capability and leaving some space to fill in their capacity for the upcoming Sprint.

Then, unsurprisingly, ask the team members if they have any leave plans or perhaps some other responsibilities that would distract them from their core duties as a Scrum Team member.

Yes, we all know as Agile practitioners that any part-time allocation of Developers to a Scrum Team is highly undesirable or might even appear "un-Agile", but we also know that it's often the reality we have to deal with. So instead of being in a sulky denial of an Agile purist, recognize this as a solid workaround and perhaps a bridging solution towards the state of increased agility.

For each team member, write down the number of days they expect to be able to contribute to this Sprint.

Having this capacity matrix at your disposal and transparently available for your whole Scrum Team to see will make the rest of your planning process more educated.

# Step 4 (*Optional*) – Establish a normalized estimation scale

For brand new Scrum Teams that don't have a historical record of their velocity, or Story Points estimation practice, and especially where capacity planning is required due to the lack of cross-functionality, it is a good idea to baseline and normalize the perception of what *1 Story Point* means to everyone.

While Story Points estimation system based on the Fibonacci sequence of numbers is intended to serve as a relative abstraction layer from the world of absolute numbers such as minutes, hours and days, it is often a good idea to rig this system in favour of making it easier to adopt among traditional software development teams.

A lot of traditional developers find it easier to estimate work effort in something more tangible, like days.

So in this optional approach that requires some suitability assessment from you as the facilitator, we will help the team drive clear parallels between the Story Points and calendar days.

I suggest using a whiteboard to write the following in large block letters at the top of it:

*1 Story Point = 1 Day of work for 1 Developer*

Explain who is classified as a "Developer" if required.

Reiterate that any work efforts you'll be calculating should be considered as "End-to-End", not just the coding part. But everything that it would take to turn a User Story into a piece of valuable functionality that's integrated with the rest of the code and possibly deployed into the required environment.

The extent of completion requirements for any piece of work should be also clearly understood and documented by the whole team in the form of the Definition of Done.

You might need to additionally clear that the work effort could be shared between the developers of the team if the Story has to exchange hands in the process if its development. You'd naturally see this happen more rarely when the Scrum Team is properly cross-functional -- when every Developer could virtually do any job -- and more often when you're dealing with the team of narrow domain specialists.

## Step 5 (*Optional*) – Establish the "Measuring Stick" User Story

Another important but optional step is to make sure the whole team understands what specific Task or User Story would serve as that mental "measuring stick" that's worth 1 day of work or 1 Story Point, before attempting to estimate the rest of the Sprint Backlog.

This is obviously applicable to situations where you as the facilitator still expect your Scrum Team to estimate work items relative to each other, rather than absolutely - with no attempted comparison to the rest of the Backlog.

It is widely known in the Agile practice that we as humans are much quicker and more accurate when sizing up things relative to one another, rather than attempting to guess the exact size of an object or duration of a certain event.

This notion is at the heart of the classic Agile estimation approach, where Story Points are used to label those relatively compared pieces of work that the development team is presented with. It ensures that no excessive guess-work is attempted, as it has no value in itself.

All we are trying to do here is guess how much we'll be able to do over the next Sprint, and then have some sort of a baseline and a system that would allow us to see the growing or decreasing performance of the whole team as the time goes by.

In order to estimate relatively regardless of the measurement units used -- Story Points or the actual Days -- the team would need to agree on what's the easiest and quickest yet not trivial piece of work that they can see in the Backlog, and could agree on labelling as a "One-pointer"?

The process of establishing this mental "measuring stick" is non-prescriptive and depends on the team culture, personalities present and established relationships. In some cases, I've seen one particular person jump up straight away and point out the Story that then was briefly discussed and agreed to be the easiest to deliver. The whole process of agreeing on the one-pointer, in that case, took less than a couple of minutes.

In other situations, the Product Owner had to scroll down the list of items in the Product Backlog that was projected on a large screen and say a few words about each and every Story and Task to give the team at least a rough idea of what those pieces of work are about, before they could decide what seemed to them as the quickest piece of work to complete.

So your mileage will vary here, but as I always say - as long as you understand the ground rules and not lose sight of the purpose of the exercise or a particular step, in this case, you should succeed.

## Step 6 - Sprint Goal nomination

Some Scrum Teams and Agile practitioners steer towards a more free-flowing format where Sprint Goals are only discussed and locked down at the end of Sprint Planning after all the work has been discussed and committed to.

I believe that if you'd be comfortable with such a free and easy approach, you wouldn't need this book that tries to give you very specific advice and instructions on how to make certain things happen.

So with that in mind, I'll say that I believe the Product Owner should always arrive at a Sprint Planning with a proposition or nomination of the Sprint Goal. After all, they have prioritized the items in the Backlog and they should know which ones are most important for the delivery of the Product Value over the next time interval.

Obviously all these preconceived priorities and the idea of a Sprint Goal would be negotiable and subject to adjustments as the whole team had a chance to discuss the work items and plan the next Sprint together. But simply not worrying about any Sprint Goal upfront and not giving your Development team any direction would not help create a positive and efficient momentum upfront, in my opinion.

Hence my suggestion for the Product Owner here is to open up with a quick pitch for what they'd like to accomplish next before the whole team even starts focusing on the individual backlog items.

I'd ask the Product Owner to write their short proposed Sprint Goal on the whiteboard, and then adjust it as required if not all of the expected work items that are needed to complete the Goal could be picked up by the team into the next Sprint.

Remind the team and the Product Owner that any goals including the Sprint Goal should be as specific and measurable as possible. I've also seen Sprint Goals with numerous outputs presented as long, comma-delimited lists. Some development environments would see that as perfectly justifiable work planning, and I'm not going to contradict that suddenly.

I'd encourage you, however, to steer towards a singular output and a Goal wherever possible as that has numerous benefits such as reduction of the context-switching, and the others.

# Step 7 - Review of the highest priority Backlog Items

The main course of any good Sprint Planning is when the Product Owner finally starts presenting the Backlog items they've nominated as most important for the next Sprint to the development team.

As I've briefly mentioned above, the ceremonies I'm recommending and describing in this book include Backlog Refinement, which normally contains a lot of the technical discussion of particular work items that the Product Owner was preparing for the upcoming Sprints.

So if you've done your Backlog Refinement already, this step of the Sprint Planning should go rather smoothly and without too much stress or time-wastage due to the development team members being familiar with the topic and perhaps even specific User Stories being presented to them.

There could be some further discussion and negotiation on the possible split of some work items into two if the developers could call out straight away that the nominated scope of work appears too large to be contained under a single Story, or clarification of the Acceptance Criteria that remain super important for the proper contract between the presenting Product Owner and the developers committing to do the work to take place.

## Step 8 - Estimation of the Backlog Items

This is where things should get interesting, as the estimation process would depend on whether or not you and your team bothered with Capacity Estimation as one of the previous steps in this process.

There are multiple Agile work estimation techniques, and I've extracted those into their separate chapters, in order to keep this one sensibly short.

Using classic Planning Poker process as a quick reference point here, I suggest keeping things simple and stick to the following routine:

1. Product Owner presents the User Story at the top of the Product Backlog and explains the reason why it's of the highest importance in their opinion.

2. The developers could ask questions about the User Story and its Acceptance Criteria, talking between themselves about how they'd turn it into the working solution.

3. Once all questions are answered and there is a consensus around the room that the requirements are understood and there are no immediately visible red flags that would prevent this User Story from being estimated, the facilitator calls for estimation.

4. The whole team picks a card (or prepares to show the number of fingers if no cards are available) representing the Fibonacci number of Story Points they believe this piece of work is worth.

As an example, a "5" would mean that the team member believes it'll take up to 5 days for one person to deliver this User Story End-to-End, given our previous step where the estimation units were agreed and normalized as 1 Point for 1 Day of work.

5. Once the numbers are revealed, the facilitator quickly summarises the result and proposes to record a number of Story Points if the votes appear consistent.

The facilitator would ask for further clarification of the Story or encourage a dialogue between the people casting the votes with a big gap between the numbers. Say, someone raised a card with "2" while another team member thought this User Story is worth an "8".

It is likely that one or another is missing some important bit of knowledge, and it's always better to ensure everyone is on the same page.

## Step 9 - Progressive update of the remaining Team capacity

This step isn't really following Step 8 as a hard sequence but is woven into the process instead, like 8-9-8-9-8-9...

Once a User Story is estimated by the team members, the Story Points need to be recorded in this particular work item. The remaining team capacity balance should be then updated to reflect that the team has committed to deliver this piece of work, deducting its estimated size from its remaining capacity.

In the case of no cross-functionality of the team, this process of voting could include some dialogue between the development team members where it becomes clear that this particular Story needs, for instance, 2 days of User Interface work, 3 days of back-end logic coding, 2 days of testing, and about 1 day worth of packaging, UAT testing, and deployment.

This is where your previously prepared Capacity Matrix of the team would become handy, and I'd suggest you capture how much capacity of the UI developer, back-end developer, and tester would be consumed individually.

While I'm aware that this turns into some kind of a precision instrument exercise, some level of it could be useful for less Agile-mature teams that are still finding their feet and require extra encouragement to take accountability for their individual capacity and commitment to deliver work.

Once some level of cross-functionality and higher maturity of Agile processes within the team is reached, this step could be loosened to simply update the number representing total capacity of the whole team, or perhaps you'd even get rid of this step altogether.

## Step 10 - Continue populating the Sprint Backlog

The estimated and accepted User Story is then transferred into the bucket of the Sprint Backlog from the Product Backlog, indicating the Team's acceptance and commitment to delivering it during the next Sprint.

This process continues until the team runs out of their pre-calculated capacity, or simply until they feel like "that's enough" for the next Sprint if you didn't bother with precise capacity calculations.

Needless to say that once the team has been sprinting for a while and has some historic velocity data on record, the process of Sprint Planning becomes much easier, with more process corners being cut as time goes on.

You'd probably stop trying to calculate team capacity every Sprint and only pay attention to major factors like the public or planned team member holidays, making adjustments to how much work the Team accepts into the Sprint.

I feel like I have to keep making references to the group of more purist Agile practitioners, who in this case would point out that everything is supposed to be high-level and relative, not attempting to be precise in capacity calculations or velocity tracking, encouraging organic and self-managing Agile approach within the Team.

While I'm perfectly aware that it's what Agile was supposed to be on paper, the harsh reality of the corporate landscape where most of these efforts would be statistically required is often different. Loosely governed yet efficient and self-directing Scrum Teams are extremely rare, and the need to provide some sort of reliable delivery forecast or retrospective analysis of Team efficiency is very common.

# Step 11 - Confirm the Sprint Goal and start the Sprint

Time to check back and confirm if the Sprint Goal that PO initially nominated for the upcoming Sprint appears feasible. It might require some rewording if not all of the Backlog Items that the PO hoped to see as part of the freshly formed Sprint Backlog were accepted by the Development team.

Have a quick discussion involving the whole Scrum team to make sure that everyone is comfortable with the Sprint Goal, that it's not too vague or broad. The basic rule of thumb that's up to personal judgment call of the facilitator and the Product Owner to uphold is that there should be a sense of common ownership and buy-into the Sprint Goal from the Development team.

After all, let's not forget the classic Scrum teaching that suggests that if the Product Owner is temporarily unavailable to make priority calls on the individual work items during the kicked off Sprint, the Development team should be able to use the Sprint Goal as their "northern star". So, ideally, reiterating the Sprint Goal should be enough for the team to autonomously decide what should be done next, even if the Product Owner is not there to guide them.

As a wrap-up of this chapter, I'd reiterate that ultimately it is up to you to decide how strict or loose you'd like your Agile practice to be. The extended process of Sprint Planning that I've offered you in this chapter, however, was successful and in most environments aspiring to be more Agile.

The variations I'm offering were generally satisfying both camps of the Agile purists, voting for less direct control over the people doing the work, and the management that didn't want to lose the sense of rigor and some sort of reliable forecasting of valuable deliverables that the team would work on.

# Chapter 3 – Daily Scrum

The most visible and recognized "heartbeat ceremony" of any Agile team is without a doubt the Daily Scrum meeting, more broadly referred to as the *Daily Stand-up*.

Due to its simplicity and shortest intended duration, the freely available Scrum Guide appears to do the best job detailing this Scrum ceremony, compared to any other that I'm covering for you in this book.

There are still different ways to run the Daily Scrum however and lots of questions that keep being asked in 2019, highlighting the need to include this information and hopefully help you figure out what you've been missing about the Daily Stand-up all along.

As per the Scrum Guide, the key purpose of the Daily Scrum is to make sure the whole Scrum Team knows what's going on and where everyone is at, as far as the committed scope of the current Sprint is concerned.

What User Stories have been started, and what's their status? Does anyone need help from the fellow team members or any clarifications from the Product Owner? Are there any blocked tasks or User Stories that require immediate attention or escalation as an impediment via the Scrum Master? What is the overall feeling among the team members about meeting the committed Sprint Goal?

These are just some of the questions that a well-run Daily Scrum meeting could answer explicitly or implicitly, by paying attention to the energy levels around the room as the facilitator or the Scrum Master of the team.

As I mentioned, there are multiple ways to run a Daily Scrum meeting, and all of those have two similar points:

1. Every team member should be given a chance to speak;
2. Try and keep the meeting to 15 minutes, encouraging the developers to take any detailed technical conversation or problem resolutions offline - continuing the conversation as a smaller group of immediately impacted developers after the official stand-up is over.

Scrum Guide description of a Daily Scrum meeting suggests that every member of the Scrum Team answers these three questions:

1. What have I been working on yesterday?
2. What will I be working on today?
3. Do I need any help and are there any blockers that I see?

Being the Agile practitioner from the trenches, I personally believe that this rigor might be necessary for brand new Scrum Teams that are still learning the Scrum ropes, but not for the teams that have some experience in Agile delivery and who know what's really going on.

For those slightly more Agile-mature teams I recommend trimming the questions to:

1. What are you working on?
2. Are you on track or need help?

I encourage to show the team the basics and be sensitive to the speed of adjustment to the new ways of working that could differ from team to team. But overall, if the team appears to be keen and not too shy to try new things and take ownership of the User Stories they raise their hand to own through the Sprint and take the lead on, letting them communicate with one another more naturally during the Daily Scrum meeting would be a good move.

Some Scrum Masters who look after larger Scrum Teams often introduce a token that is passed around from person to person, indicating who has the right of speech at any point in time. This is supposed to help people focus and not interrupt each other when giving updates.

While the whole practice makes me cringe a bit as I'm always after treating people like responsible adults rather than a bunch of children who choose to rely on superficial rituals to keep themselves in check, I have seen fairly immature Agile-aspiring environments where passing a whiteboard marker actually improved adoption of the whole practice.

Another common question on the topic of running an efficient Daily Scrum meeting is who is allowed to attend? The answer is - anyone, as long as they understand the ground rule of chickens and the pigs.

I don't know how many times this story was told in many variants, but I'll give you my own quick version explaining this de-facto rule of an Agile Daily Scrum attendance etiquette:

A Chicken suggested to a Pig that they open a bacon and egg breakfast place up the road. Pig thought about it for a while and said - "*No, I think I'll pass*". Chicken asked - "*Why not?*" Pig answered - "*I appear to be a lot more invested than you!*"

I remember the times when this story wasn't as overused and corny sounding as it probably does to my reader in 2019, but the moral of it is still crystal clear. The Scrum Team members are the ones committed to achieving the Sprint Goal. The guests and observers of the Daily Scrum could be interested in the results and having some stake in the whole Product delivery game, but they aren't actually putting any delivery efforts into the process, so they should remain respectfully silent.

Another very common misconception surrounding the Daily Scrum meeting is that it's an update to the Scrum Master or the Program

Manager or some other senior stakeholder who decided to show up on time.

It is your responsibility as the facilitator to ensure that any attendees understand the simple rules of this meeting and the purpose. Which is for the development team to make sure they are on track to their target, rather than digressing into answering questions from the Project Manager who whoever else from the outside of the Scrum Team on why perhaps something is blocked or isn't being delivered as quickly as they hoped.

There are opportunities to inspect the results of the work Scrum Team does during the Sprint, provide feedback and ask any questions they like - during the Sprint Review session. You as the facilitator or the actual Scrum Master of the team should be able to quickly explain that in the friendliest and encouraging manner.

Keeping things real here however, I'll tell you about a situation where the CEO of a large Australian Telecommunications company was once on the floor where one of my Scrum Teams was doing their Daily Scrum. So the CEO stopped nearby, just behind the backs of the circle of my Scrum Team members and simply listened until everyone gave their updates, and then made their presence visible to others - causing a few nervous laughs - and asked a couple of basic questions about how the team was feeling and if they needed any of the senior Leadership support.

I trust you to have the emotional intelligence necessary to recognize any similar "attendance" of someone from the outside of the Scrum Team as a greater good situation, and not attempt to stop the CEO from talking or try and explain some rules to them...

Everything we do as Agile practitioners has a greater picture and longer-term horizon in mind.

A viewpoint more familiar to Transformation Leaders and Agile Coaches, rather than a hypothetical fresh Scrum Master, one should try and see that a little disruption of one Scrum ceremony is insignificant compared to the greater effect of a senior Leader showing their support and encouragement to the team to keep going and adopt the new ways of working.

In Lean practice this is known as the Leadership "*Gemba*" Walk, where senior management and leaders are encouraged to go to the actual place where the work is being done, to observe how that value is being produced and speak with the real people on the ground, rather than remain locked up in their ivory tower and a clean boardroom, surrounded by abstract report numbers and graphs.

This topic goes way beyond the scope of what I've intended to cover in this book, but I decided to give you this perspective as the ultimate purpose of what I'm writing here is to make you into a more all-rounded and mature Agile practitioner, whichever exact role you might have.

# Chapter 4 – Sprint Review

Widely known by its street name, Sprint Review or the Showcase is one of those non-negotiable Scrum ceremonies that need to happen even if it's rain or a hail storm outside, in my opinion.

As with all other Scrum-originating ceremonies, a Sprint Review is there not just to inspect the Product Increment that the sum of all the delivered parts adds up to at the end of the current Sprint. This event also helps us ensure that the Business stakeholders and any other Customer-proxies get a sense of the Agile delivery heartbeat that you as facilitator help maintain, getting an opportunity to meet the team and provide their feedback.

Using the term "Showcase" that's certainly known much more widely than the "Sprint Review" did more damage to the Agile practice across the landscape of corporate Digital Delivery than one might realize. Calling it a Showcase and helping propagate this term among the Business stakeholders, Leaders of various levels and the Executives of the companies implicitly generates an expectation that the Scrum team is just there to show what they've done.

I spoke to many people acting in different roles who had absolutely no idea that the ultimate goal of a Sprint Review is not just to show, but to encourage the conversation with those who are interested in receiving the finished Product at the end of the day, who might have useful and constructive feedback to provide to the Product Owner.

The Product Owner then could take it or leave it, put simply, but at least they'd be given a chance to manage expectations of the people who are potentially paying for the whole show, as part of a properly done Scrum process, rather than by giving into the requirement of providing some other traditional Project reports and Steering Committee updates.

So with the purpose of the event out of the way, let's get through the recommended process that you could tweak as required to make it fit better into the specific structure of your organization.

## Step 1 - Ensure that Business stakeholders are attending

As I said in the introduction chapter of this book, I won't stop and explain the obvious fact that the "right people" need to attend your ceremonies. In this case, however, I have to reiterate this, as it's probably the main ceremony that's rendered almost useless if those right people aren't participating or even knowing that they are invited at all.

Product Owner should invite the Product Manager and the Business Owner, as well as the key Business stakeholders to attend this recurring Scrum ceremony. Do not assume that those people understand what the ceremony is about and why their attendance is highly desirable, so perhaps an informal meeting and explanation of what to expect from the Sprint Review would be in order.

Yet again, the point I'm making above won't be explicitly required if the whole part of the organization undergoing a pivot towards agility had an appropriate level of Agile Fundamentals training. In any case, it would be a good idea for you to confirm while ensuring that your Scrum team is set up for success.

A common question is if the Sprint Review should happen if none of the Business stakeholders could or wanted to attend?

The short answer is - yes, it should. The logic here is that if the campfire is burning, it might eventually be noticed and attract some visitors, helping establish this feel of the new and collaborative ways of working.

In this case of Business non-attendance or disinterest, you have bigger problems than knowing how to run the ceremony properly. As an Agile Coach I'd see a myriad of problems stemming off this unsupportive attitude, where the Information Technology people would be left to their own devices to "be Agile", while Business effectively won't commit to playing ball with everyone and just continue issuing their requirements the traditional way, by throwing those over the wall.

If you notice this type of push-back or simply lacking momentum of Business participation in Sprint Reviews and any other activities they are welcome to at least attend as observers, I'd suggest that you raised it with your Agile Coach or Agile Transformation Leadership of any kind.

While I assume that in the majority of cases you as my reader would be most likely a Scrum Master or another immediate member of the Scrum Team, trying to facilitate these ceremonies and activities, someone with potentially a higher level of organizational influence would need to help you champion this cause of changing the ways the departments work together.

Without this collaboration and voluntary participation of Business representatives in the Information Technology-driven delivery activities you basically don't have the foundational setup that will allow your organization to become more Agile.

## Step 2 - Product Owner opens the meeting

Another very common question is who should be actually facilitating the ceremony and "doing most of the talking"?

The short answer is - any Scrum Team member can facilitate the ceremony, but it usually falls on the Scrum Master or the Product Owner.

Regardless of who is doing the facilitation, it is up to the Product Owner to open the meeting and tell the audience about the goals that the team has set to achieve over the Sprint in review. This is where it comes to the individual skills of public speaking and presenting, where the format is loose and non-prescriptive.

Generally, I'd recommend that the Product Owner quickly recaps the Sprint Goal, and might choose to quickly show the Sprint Backlog with the most prominent User Stories or items that highlight the pieces of functionality that will be demonstrated by the team during this session.

For example, the Product Owner could open this meeting with the following little speech:

"*Hi everyone,*

*I'm the Product Owner of the Frontend Awesomeness team, welcome to our Sprint 7 Review.*

*For this Sprint our main goal was to deliver the updated web User Interface for the Customer Dashboard. We took twenty User Stories into this Sprint, with a couple of those highlighting the key functionality we'll be demonstrating to you today...*

*Now I'll hand over to John, one of our Developers to show you what awesome features we've managed to complete!*"

It is generally seen as a good and Team-empowering practice to not keep talking through the whole Review session but delegate to the Developers to demonstrate the features they've been taking a lead on.

Sometimes the demonstration could be limited to one of the Developers on a rotational basis to present all of the delivered features. But more commonly the screen-sharing is done by two or three Developers to make sure everyone gets a chance to shine.

Needless to say that especially while you're teaching the team how to run their Sprint Reviews, this process could appear a little awkward or clunky as you pass the ball around the room and the Developers connect their devices to the projector they demonstrate their work on, but this phase usually passes pretty quickly and the presentations vastly improve over time.

All teams find their own groove and method of presenting the materials that work best for them and their stakeholders.

# Step 3 - the Developers present the delivered functionality

It is always recommended to present something that works, even if not all the real data sources or other elements of the solution that make it "real" are connected or properly working yet. Ideally, Scrum recommends that when you present something that's fully complete and working perfectly, making it a "Potentially Shippable Increment" of your Product.

But the reality is often quite different, and my goal is to make sure that my book doesn't sound like another picture-perfect guide. What I'd like to do instead is to prepare you for those awkward and imperfect situations that our lives as Scrum Masters and other Agile champion roles are filled with.

So when the Scrum Team couldn't deliver a perfectly independently shippable piece of the solution, you still should find a way to demonstrate it to the stakeholders, showing the value that's being progressively and iteratively built in the background.

Which is why even if the team couldn't turn the results of this Sprint into a fully self-contained and shippable package, but instead produced some new functionality or output that could only be deployed to User Acceptance Testing (UAT) environment rather than Production, you should encourage the team to demonstrate that as the achievement, instead of shying away and coming across as having nothing to show.

And hopefully needless to say that having something to demonstrate in the Development or Testing environments that still gives the stakeholders a good idea of what your Scrum kitchen is currently cooking, would be always seen more favourably than a few PowerPoint slides that don't show real functionality or Customer value.

## Step 4 - Product Owner accepts the work and asks for feedback

This step does not have to be strictly sequential and once again might take many forms, depending on the relationship of the team with the audience, the nature of work and other particulars of your organization.

Not strictly sequential means that in many cases the Product Owner already accepted the work that the team has completed as Done, not having to formally acknowledge their satisfaction with the results in front of an audience. One could also say why would the team demonstrate something that they are not confident in, as even their own Product Owner hasn't accepted yet?

Answering that question and choosing what works for you is unsurprisingly up to you and your team, yet again.

The important part of this step is to address the invited Business stakeholders and any other Customer segment representatives and ask them for their impressions and feedback. While I'd take a moment to do this in any case, most of the Sprint Reviews I've been facilitating had the format where I encouraged the audience to ask questions or provide feedback during the show, not necessarily waiting until the end.

Some people choose to collect their thoughts and see the whole presentation become coming up with feedback and suggestions, while others would forget what they wanted to say in one particular moment, so encouraging them to feel as informal and welcome as possible usually leads to a better long-term relationship and atmosphere of the ceremony as a whole.

What kind of feedback could come from the Business stakeholders at this stage?

Frankly, anything that they might find helpful to highlight to the team and the Product Owner specifically. Wherever possible, we should try and encourage the attendees to be positive rather than sounding dissatisfied and disappointed, to keep the positive momentum going for the team.

This is not to say that everyone should try and seem chirpy and excited if something that the team is showing is far below the initially set expectations or the original Sprint goal. Agile ceremonies are a fine balancing act of putting collaboration and transparency first, but not digress into making things personal or frustrating for everyone involved, if things didn't go according to plan.

Upfront acknowledgment of the fact that the original expectations might be higher than what the team was able to achieve due to clearly stated factors that might have held the team's progress back could go a long way before commencing the demonstration.

Everything we do as Agile champions and facilitators of those ceremonies, in this case, is subject to the development of emotional intelligence that would help you choose the best direction and ensure that your ceremony runs smoother while achieving its primary goals.

Usually, the best way for the Product Owner to handle feedback is to acknowledge and take note of everything that the Business stakeholders decided to share on the spot.

We assume that the Product Owner would have some ongoing relationship with the attendees of the Sprint Review, so there shouldn't really be any drastic pieces of feedback that would throw everyone off or make the Product Owner rethink their whole approach to the Product strategy. After all, the PO would have been catching up with the Business offline and during their solo Backlog refinement efforts, so the chances of Business being really surprised or thrown off by whatever the team is presenting should be pretty low.

Still, one thing is talking about something in theory, and another - seeing the newly developed functionality as a Product feature. This is why even the people you've spoken to as a PO many times might have lots of suggestions and questions or even less popular comments like "*Oh... I've imagined this completely differently...*"

The key to becoming better at running Business-facing ceremonies such as the Sprint Review is preparation.

You could choose to briefly discuss what the team will be comfortable to demonstrate during a regular Backlog Refinement session or even straight after your regular Daily Scrum. Keep in mind that the time you'd then expect the team to spend preparing for the Sprint Review should be spent very conservatively. The team should never have to start working for presentation's sake.

As with most things in the Agile process, it is a balancing act. Fresh teams are typically not as good at it as more well-established and mature Agile practitioner groups would be.

If the Definition of Done and the rest of the Scrum process that your team is exercising are held to a satisfactory standard, in theory, you should have everything more or less ready for the Sprint Review.

Just need to book a room that would fit all the invitees, have a projector or a screen large enough to present whichever Product features the team was ready to deliver, and the willing group of participants.

# Chapter 5 – Retrospectives

An Agile Retrospective is not just one of the best-known ceremonies across the companies delivering some form of Digital Services or Products but is also one of the most frequently used outside of any formal Agile methodology or process, such as Scrum.

We'll still refer to the Scrum Guide here though, reiterating that a Retrospective is intended to allow the Scrum team to inspect itself, and have an honest chat between the team members about how things went and what could be improved going forward.

Every Agile ceremony, as you surely would have figured by now, has multiple ways to run it, as people adopt the practice and improvise a lot. In this chapter, I'll talk to you about the two most basic ways to run a Retro, basing your choice around the scale of your team.

We'll start by going through the steps and particulars of a Scrum-team sized Retrospective.

# **Step 1 -** Make sure the whole Scrum team participates

A common question is who should participate in a Retro, and specifically if the Product Owner should be there? The answer is that it's a Scrum-team focused ceremony, so the whole Scrum team including the Product Owner and Scrum Master should be there.

Another question I get all the time if any managers should be able to participate too - the Project or Program Manager supporting the Agile initiative perhaps. The answer is no, they should not, as this would interfere with the purpose of the meeting.

Team-focused Retrospective is a safe environment to speak your mind and complain if someone wishes to, and then openly discuss the frustration someone might be experiencing without any fear of management hearing them and perhaps becoming defensive or vindictive.

It's pointless to argue about such behaviours or reactions being unwelcome in most modern corporate environments, as the fact is that people will always remain people. And a developer who is frustrated with management and isn't well-versed in public speaking and expressing their frustration would likely either not express their concern at all in front of a manager, or phrase it in an edgy way that they might regret later.

Your job as the facilitator is to ensure that all the participants and the supporting management understand the purpose of a Team-focused Retrospective, respecting the rules and giving the team a chance to vent in private if they choose to.

# Step 2 - Prepare the Retro board

Some people refer to it as the Wall, as most Retrospectives end up with a bunch of Post-It notes stuck to some kind of a wall or a whiteboard. The Board or the Wall are not literal sometimes, as I've seen pretty successful use of a large desk or a few of those pushed together to create a large flat surface that the Post-Its could be placed on when there's no vertical Wall or a window available.

Regardless of your surface choice, I recommend that you create one of the following two sets of columns that will determine the rest of the process:

- Start
- Stop
- Continue
- Actions

Or an even more straightforward format:

- What went well?
- What could be improved?
- Actions

The first set of columns suggests that you as the facilitator would then ask the whole team to spend a few minutes writing their thoughts on the Post-It notes, answering the following questions:

*"What should we start doing as a Team to improve our performance and wellbeing?"*
*"What should we stop doing, as it didn't work for us or has a bad impact on the Team?"*
*"What did you enjoy doing as part of the Team and think we should keep doing?"*

The second proposed column format is even more self-explanatory, as you're basically diving straight in and asking the team members to focus on two main questions:

*"What do you think went well for us as a Team over the past Sprint? Something we should do more of, and celebrate!"*
*"What didn't work, should be stopped or improved if we have to keep doing it?"*

Leave the Actions column alone for now and tell the team that you'll get to it once the other columns have been filled and the whole team had a chance to discuss everyone's thoughts and ideas.

# Step 3 - Let the team capture their thoughts

As the team is writing their Post-It notes, encourage them to walk up to the Wall and stick them there when they are ready. It is normally recommended to not comment yet but to keep paying attention to what people are writing. As the facilitator, you'd try and group similar thoughts, ideas, and suggestions into clusters.

If you use a large whiteboard, you could simply stick those similar Post-its together, and draw a large circle around those, to determine and label a "theme" that would be easier to focus on and discuss later.

If you can't draw on the wall or the flat surface of your choosing, I'd suggest that you simply stick the Post-It notes over each other, or like a little trailing "branch" that would be easy enough to isolate as a cluster for further discussion.

The timing of this step normally depends on the size of the team or specific circumstances that would clearly need more time to be properly reflected in the team's written up thoughts.

So you should determine this on the spot as the facilitator of the ceremony in the room. I've seen writing of the notes to be as short

as 10 minutes, or stretch beyond 20 for larger teams in the state
of transformational crisis.

# Step 4 - Facilitate the discussion

The longest, and arguably most important part of any
Retrospective is the discussion of the key themes and thoughts
that the team members have put up on the Wall.

I always recommend starting with the positives, explaining to the
team that while we'd ultimately like to focus on the improvement of
things that didn't go so well, it is important to acknowledge the
wins and give each other a well-deserved pat on the back.

This is where you'd read out and discuss what's been captured in
the "Start" and "Continue", or "What went well?" columns.

When I facilitate the Team-focused Retrospectives, I would have
already grouped all the prominent themes and singled out the
"loudest" individual thoughts for discussion. You'd generally get a
feel for someone's frustration or need to express themselves and
be heard. It is usually a good idea to address those positive or
negative outbursts.

Even if there were no more than one Post-It note with such a flash
of personal opinion, sometimes those are worth reading out loud
and acknowledging, or even encouraging a brief discussion

around the room. This is mainly to make sure the issue or thought was properly addressed and not left to fester in the background.

*"What do you guys think about this thought? Would the author of this Post-It like to elaborate on this further? Do we have anyone else who agrees or disagrees?"*

Efficient facilitation of a discussion that allows people to be heard, leading to a common understanding, dousing of the flames that might be burning in the background, or helping the group come to a consensus and an Action that would potentially resolve the issue or situation that was brought up takes skill and practice.

Even a targeted guide like this one wouldn't be able to tell you exactly what to say or do, as you'd need to exercise the emotional intelligence, observe and listen to the group of people, nudging the discussion towards a solution where possible, and making sure every side gets a chance to speak and chip in.

When you've moved on to "What could be improved?" notes, your main goal shifts to facilitating a discussion where everyone feels heard, concerns are acknowledged or politely questioned by the other team members, and the team generates ideas that could lead to resolution of the identified problems.

Some issues could be resolved by the Scrum team itself, hence this opportunity for the whole team to inspect itself! Those are usually the easiest to deal with and produce clear Actions for.

Actions are captured on Post-It notes as a brief indication of what the team agrees to do to address whatever it is that someone wrote up on the "unhappy" Wall. Perhaps not as obvious as we'd like to think, any Action should have a voluntary assignee - someone who will take the lead on making sure this action comes to fruition, resolving the identified issue.

## Example Scenario #1

In this scenario we imagine a situation that the team could agree to try and resolve on their own, without any escalations or asking for external help.

Mary writes - "*I feel like we shouldn't commit to as much work as we've tried to take on during the last Sprint. We were too ambitious and didn't meet the Sprint goal. This doesn't make me feel good.*"

The team discusses this point and agrees that they've probably been too stretched by the large size of the Sprint Backlog and not meeting the Sprint Goal doesn't feel great.

The proposed Action that their Scrum Master takes a lead on is to "*Ensure that we reduce the number of Story Points we aim to deliver during the next Sprint by 20% to find our comfortable velocity again.*"

The team does not need any external help to try and fix the identified issue. They choose to make adjustments and experiment with the new indicative capacity, and the Scrum Master is tasked to keep a close eye on the team's commitment, keeping it in check.

## Example Scenario #2

Where the team needs help of a role with external stakeholder access:

John writes - "*I feel like there's too much interference from the Business during the Sprint, trying to get us to work on the things we haven't committed to do. As a Developer, I feel like I can't keep saying no to the people paying for this show. It makes me frustrated!*"

The team is encouraged to discuss this pretty clear issue, and the general consensus is that in fact, this is what happens frequently to the development team members.

Business stakeholders don't recognize the presence of a Product Owner in the area or the new rules of the game where every piece of work has to be captured, made visible in the Product Backlog and the team Agile Wall, and prioritized.

So the proposed action that Dmitri as an Agile Coach of the Team is happy to take a lead on is to "Engage with the Head of Marketing and offer an explanation and training in how Agile Scrum teams of IT are working, to ensure transparency and timely completion of the committed work".

Will this Action solve the issue?

The team could only guess at this stage, but it's an educated guess where seeking an understanding and sponsorship from a senior stakeholder of the department causing this disruption could lead to them explaining the new rules of engagement to their direct reports, helping everyone to come to an understanding.

# Program-level Retrospectives

For larger teams or the whole Programs of work, we change the Retrospective format a little further. The main differences are in the attempt to funnel the thoughts of the broad team into specific areas of potential celebration or improvement for the company.

So your Retro Board or the Wall could be divided into the following column headings, sometimes accompanied with a little text or bullet-points explaining further what thoughts should go there.

In any case and due to the much larger scale of this ceremony, you'd create the two Walls - a "Happy" Wall, and an "Unhappy"

One. Naturally, the thoughts of what went well would go on the happy wall, while the unhappy one will capture areas for improvement.

Each wall would have the same "Funnels" prepared. For example:

- Team & People
- Process
- Resourcing
- Tools & Systems
- Enterprise Architecture
- Other, Miscellaneous

Then the facilitator would divide the room of participants in half, asking one of those halves to work on the "Happy" wall, while others fill out the "Unhappy" side. I'd ask these groups to swap sides after 20 minutes so that everyone gets a chance to contribute.

The discussion part of this format could take longer, with the facilitator playing back to the group what they've heard from everyone when discussing the key identified themes and issues, capturing those themes concisely for further ideation.

## Ideation Step - Team breakouts

Once again due to a much larger scale of such a Program-wide Retrospective, it's common to then ask the larger group to break into smaller teams of up to five people, where each group takes one of the key themes or issues to discuss.

The goal here is for each one of those groups to discuss the theme or topic they've selected to ideate on, and come up with suggestions or a proposed list of actions that might be required to resolve the identified issue.

For example:

One of the areas of improvement that the larger team identified and discussed during the debrief following the Post-It notes writing step could have been "*Reduce the impact of BAU work on our capacity across the board*".

So a small group of 5 people who felt most strongly about the disruption "Business-As-Usual" work causes to Scrum teams have volunteered to lead the ideation process surrounding this issue.

Everyone takes another 10 minutes to go into their corners or even out of the Retrospective room for a little bit of quiet discussion space, where they have a chat about the issue, share ideas between themselves, and write down a few bullet points they prepare to present to the rest of the larger group when they return.

In 10-15 minutes time, the facilitator calls everyone back into the Retro room, and the BAU ideation group volunteers to present their ideas and proposed actions first.

John goes up to the front of the room and tells everyone:

*"We've been discussing the issues surrounding the disruption we feel across our teams from the BAU work requests that keep pouring in without any respect to our capacity or committed Sprint Goals. We all recognize the importance of BAU to "keep the lights on", but the negative impact of it can't be denied."*

*"So we are proposing,"* John continues, *"the following few actions that we'd hope to get some assistance of our Tribe Leadership from..."*

And then John might list a few sensible things to try, like:

1. Communicate to the rest of the organization how the transformed Agile Delivery streams of the IT are working, to reduce confusion among Business stakeholders;

2. Advertise the right ways to engage with the IT Operational streams of work that are designed to handle BAU requests, so that the Project or Initiative delivery streams aren't impacted in any way;

3. Request the Tribe Leadership to revisit the staffing strategy and recognize the need to recruit and on-board new specialists required to handle BAU-specific requests...

This presentation concludes with the rest of the group chiming in, perhaps asking questions or suggesting different solutions to the existing issue. As the facilitator, you'd do well to drive this part towards its logical conclusion where specific actions are recorded and owners of those actions assigned.

Once the actions are recorded - as clear, achievable and measurable results that are believed to improve the problems in review - this technically concludes your Retrospective and the wrap-up, debrief and thanking the participants is left largely up to you.

I hope this gives you a good idea of what this part is about and how this conversation could go. The ability of you as a facilitator to turn this rough outline into a good process is what will differentiate more mature practitioners from those who are only just learning the ropes.

But the good news is as always that we've all started somewhere, and most of us have gotten better over time!

# Chapter 6 – Games and Energizers

Having discussed all the main Agile ceremonies that mostly come to us from Scrum Framework and probably cover close to 80% of the activities happening on the ground during an Agile Transformation, I thought I'd offer you a little bonus chapter, talking about Energizer exercises.

Energizers are usually the Team warm-up and ice-breaker activities that usually an Agile Coach or a Trainer includes as part of their lengthier collaboration sessions and workshops.

While the running frequency and the choice of an Energizer are very much up to the facilitator, as a rule of thumb I'd recommend including one of those for every couple of hours that required some serious work and concentration from your team.

Typical occasions when running a little Energizer might be a good idea could include:

- Before starting a lengthy workshop, as an Ice-Breaker;
- As an opportunity for the team to refocus and re-energize after sitting for a while during a training session or a workshop;
- **Used more carefully** - if you sense that a "hard reset" is required to close off some contentious topic that was

discussed as part of a Retrospective or Discovery, or reduce the tension around the group.

Picking the right Energizer and throwing those into the process intelligently, sensing the audience rather than relying on hard-planned agendas are all the skills and behaviours that would differentiate a more experienced facilitator from someone relatively junior in their role.

This most likely would sound daunting to you, especially if you've never suggested or facilitated Energizer activities with your team. One rule of thumb I'll offer you here to ease you into the practice of using Energizers is to **not overdo it**.

So if your team event has a duration of two hours or longer, chances are one Energizer that fits your audience would be a good idea. I wouldn't add any further ones until you are comfortable with sensing your audience a bit better and are more confident in choosing the right break-up activity out of the selection of available ones.

There are few things more annoying than an overzealous fresh Agile Coach who insists on doing all sorts of Agile games and activities every 30 minutes of some training session. Trust me, I've witnessed many of those and with very few exceptions, it usually turned into quite a horror of an experience for the participants...

Don't become that kind of facilitator!

Final thought here before we jump into the descriptions of specific Agile games, Energizers, Ice-Breakers or whatever the term you prefer to describe those little activities:

Whether or not you feel like you are at the stage of being able to quickly determine if an Energizer or two would be a good idea for a specific Team event, I could almost guarantee that having one or two up your sleeve is better than only knowing the bare-bones mandatory ceremonies of Scrum!

# Energizer 1 - Something in common

## When to use?

One of the easiest to explain and facilitate Ice-Breakers out there, "Something in common" works best among the groups of people who haven't worked together before but would be expected to collaborate in some way as part of a larger event that you're running.

Typical scenarios I could picture here would include the moment after greeting your audience as part of an all-day training activity, where you'd suggest to quickly play this before jumping into the planned content of the session. As the name of the Energizer suggests, this is a very simple activity allowing people to get to know each other a little better, and generally feel more comfortable working together on the upcoming training tasks or activities.

## Recommended timing

Up to 10 minutes.

## Process

- Ask everyone to stand up;
- Tell the participants to turn to the person on their right;
- Encourage them to have a quick chat with the goal to find out one unusual or simply unexpected thing they might have in common;
- Optionally they should feel free to share their random findings with the larger group.

# Energizer 2 – The Human Map

## When to use?

This activity works best when you have larger audiences and more space to occupy. It's also a little longer than the first energizer we've looked at above, so you as facilitator might want to suggest it when you simply have more time to fill as part as an all-day workshop, team event or training activity.

## Recommended timing

Up to 20 minutes.

## Process

Depending on the scale of your event and the total number of participants, you could choose to run this as a whole larger group, or to suggest breaking down into smaller groups of 5-10 members and then playing this game within each individual group of people.

- Tell the participants that the intent is to create a human map of where each member of the group is originally from;
- Ask the participants to stand up, and find a large enough open area around the room where their map will be created;
- Then the group should agree where the center of their map will be, virtually representing the city everyone is currently in;

- Find a way to indicate the North, East, South and West. If the game is played in smaller groups, this decision could be made between all the playing teams, so that the look of each created human map is somewhat consistent in the end;
- Encourage the participants to stand on the floor around the central point, positioning themselves in a way best highlighting where they come from. The further away from the central point, the further away the city or country where the person might be coming from actually is;
- Optionally ask someone to take a photo, preferably from an elevated position, to give everyone a sense of joy and participation in a larger event that will hopefully bring back warm memories later!

# Energizer 3 - "High Five" or "Pat on the Back"

## When to use?

A mini-energizer that should be used sparingly as a virtual "explanation mark", basically telling people that certain activity is complete, and they should just breathe out and cheer for themselves for doing well! Mini-energizers are tempting to throw in here and there during lengthy workshops and training sessions, but you should be mindful about not overdoing those as the crowd will just start rolling their eyes at you.

As this book focused on the key Agile ceremonies plus a few of these additional Agile energizers, I won't go through the content that I'm planning for the next book which will include optional and advanced activities and Agile Training Games, such as the Scrum Lego game, Paper Airplane Building exercise, Kanban Coin Flip, Kanban Pizza game or similar activities designed to teach the audience something, rather than just break ice or serve as a warm-up.

I'm mentioning those activities here, as even without any detail provided for those, I could use them as great examples of something that could be nicely followed by a quick "High Five" exclamation mark.

## Recommended timing

2-5 minutes.

## Process

- Pick the right moment to ask your audience to do this! It could be framed by the facilitator as – "We've just finished *this activity and you've all collaborated so well, nice work! Time to stretch our legs for a minute… Let's all stand up!"*

- Everyone stands up…
- Tell the audience to quickly high-five two random people next to them!

## "Pat on the back" variant

If you feel like this worked well the first time and caused a few smiles and laughs around the room, you might want to run this little energizer a second time, after diving into some other training topic or workshop segment for a couple of hours perhaps.

This time it would be a good idea to switch it up a little, so that it doesn't seem too repetitive for the participants and instead of asking them to high-five their colleagues, you'd ask them to give the person next to them a pat on the back.

I have to say that due to the sensitivity of the modern society, when you encourage any tactile type of interaction between the participants of your workshops – even something as innocent as this – you should be aware of how formal is the meeting and general culture of the organisation and teams that you're working with, adjusting your approach and suggested energizer variants accordingly.

# Energizer 4 - "Rock, Paper, Scissors"

## When to use?

Similar situations to the ones described above – longer workshops, training sessions, team events where a quick switch of context and activity could help everyone refocus, before you proceed to the next topic or activity on the agenda. This activity could be run in a shorter format, or a longer "elimination" format when you have more time to fill as an all-day workshop facilitator or trainer.

## Recommended timing

10 – 20 minutes, depending on the chosen format.

## Process – shorter version

- Ask the group to break up into random pairs of people
- Pairs play the game of Rock, Paper, Scissors
- Best 2 out of 3 - wins the bragging rights!

## Process – longer "Elimination" version

- Ask the group to break up into pairs
- Pairs play the game of Rock, Paper, Scissors
- Best 2 out of 3 is the winner of the pair
- The winners should raise their right hand in the air, making it easier for other winners to find them
- The winners form random new pairs and play the game again
- The games continue until only one winner remains
- The ultimate winner gets even bigger bragging rights!

# Energizer 5 - "Your Superpower"

## When to use?

Training exercises, during a break in the lecture, as a quick ice-breaker between the people who might have never worked together before.

This little game also works very well with the teams that know each other, for example as a starter or closure of a Retrospective session. Knowing your team-mates allows you to have more laughs with them in general when you try and tell them how your ability to fly actually beats their invisibility.

If introduced at the end of a more serious and work-related workshop, this might help people leave smiling and on a more positive note than only thinking about specific tasks they perhaps had to now deal with.

## Recommended timing

Up to 10 minutes.

## Process

- Everyone is encouraged to stand up and break into random pairs
- Encourage the participants to have a chat about what super-power they'd like to have and why?
- Encourage active listening from the participants, where it's supposed to be a fun process challenging your partner in a friendly way by questioning if they think their power is better than yours, and how?
- Feel free to share the most unusual or funniest stories and discoveries that people might have had as part of the exercise with the larger audience to have a laugh and relax

further, before going back to more serious and professional training or workshop topics.

# Energizer 6 - "Untangle Yourselves"

## When to use?

This is a physical warm-up exercise that switches the audience from comprehending the offered content - usually a lengthy training material. Encourages problem-solving as a team, and working together while lifting the spirits and causing some awkward giggles.

Requires a certain level of sensitivity and knowledge of the company and team culture before being suggested to the participants. Not everyone might be comfortable with close proximity or breaking the boundaries of personal space, which should be taken seriously.

If you think the exercise would be fun for the majority of the potential participants, at the very least make it clear that participation is strictly optional and if anyone is uncomfortable with how the game is to be played, they can sit it out with no questions asked.

## Recommended timing

Up to 15 minutes.

## Process

- If you have a large audience - break them out into smaller teams of 5-10 people;
- Ask them to form a circle;
- Give the tangling instructions:

  - With your right hand, grab someone's left hand;
  - With your left hand, grab someone's right hand;
  - You cannot grab the hands of the people next to you!

- Now ask the groups to untangle themselves without letting the hands go, trying to go back to a perfect circle that they've started in.

Needless to say that there are a lot more Agile Energizers and Ice-Breaker games out there, and you are most welcome to Google for more, to enrich your personal knowledge base of these activities further, and use them smartly where appropriate!

# Conclusion

There are many ways to run your typical Agile ceremonies, most of which are originating from the Scrum Framework.

Some of the true Agile practitioners would argue that there's never a "wrong" way either since the key objective is to experiment and learn with your Scrum Team, not trying to be perfect or precisely correct the first time you do something.

In reality, however, everyone would look to you for guidance, as their local Agile champion and someone who should know how things need to be done. In many cases, it would detract from your image of an experienced Scrum Master or a bearer of another important Agile role if you show hesitation and the lack of experience conducting those ceremonies.

As I often bring this back to the job market competition, being one of the most realistic and relevant motivators for self-education, someone who knows how to do certain things in practice would always win over someone who does not.

I sincerely hope that the information offered in this book would give you an additional competitive edge, helping you land better in the role of a fresh Scrum Master or another champion of a local Agile process.

Your feedback, questions and further content requests are most welcome as always, and my contact details are in the section below.

If you are seeking further and perhaps more advanced knowledge of Lean-Agile practices, you might want to follow me on LinkedIn, Twitter or YouTube for the announcements of the upcoming JoinAgile publications that are currently in the making.

\*\*\*

# Please Review the Book!

Social validation is everything these days, so the biggest compliment for me would be your quick rating and/or a couple of lines of review **on Amazon.com**. Please spare a few minutes to visit the eBook page on Amazon and leave your rating or review!

# Audiobook version

If you prefer to listen to the audio version of this content, I intend to publish an audiobook shortly following publication of this eBook.

As inclusion of the direct link was not possible when I was preparing this manuscript, I encourage you to either visit http://JoinAgile.com for the updates and links to the latest publications, or search for the book title directly on http://Audible.com or on your preferred audiobook retailer website.

If the audiobook can't be found there just yet, it means that publishing and approval processes are still happening, and it should be listed shortly. Please check back, and I sincerely appreciate your interest and support of this initiative by being one of my readers and listeners!

# JoinAgile on YouTube

Most of my social activity in 2019 is either in LinkedIn posts, or on **JoinAgile YouTube Channel** that I'd like you to visit and consider subscribing to.

# "Get Hired as Scrum Master" Book

If you haven't read it yet, but are actively seeking to progress your career from one of the more traditional Project delivery positions towards Agile roles, this earlier publication of mine could be of help and interest to you:

**"Get Hired As Scrum Master"** - https://www.amazon.com/GET-HIRED-SCRUM-MASTER-Transitioning-ebook/dp/B01I1OVEV0

This book was written for the job applicants who have decided to take their very first steps towards Agile Project Management and Digital Delivery professional space, transitioning from other roles, and aspiring to become Scrum Masters.

We saw a lot of professionals change their jobs from Software Developers, Business Analysts, Project Managers, Technical Team Leaders and others to some form of Agile Delivery professionals such as Scrum Masters over the past few years.

I've been through this process myself, learning first-hand what works and what doesn't when it comes to breaching the "Wall of Recruiters" that usually stand between you and that job of a Scrum Master that you might desire. The influx of competing applicants is so large - *at least in the Australian job market of 2016-2019* - that you'd be severely reducing your chances of being shortlisted for job interviews and getting hired if you are not trying to be ahead of the crowd.

Lack of specific knowledge about how Agile job market works, how to properly prepare yourself and your professional Resume, how to handle Agile interview questions appropriately, what specific knowledge and experience to build up is what would be holding you back.

Written primarily for aspiring professionals who want to enter the world of Agile Project Management and Digital Delivery, but who do not possess the right knowledge or insights yet, "**Get Hired as Scrum Master**" is my attempt to share my personal findings and summarize research made as part of becoming a Professional Scrum Master.

You'll read plenty of my subjective but educated opinions on a number of topics surrounding general theme of presenting yourself as the most appealing Agile job candidate, receiving advice on how to work with your current professional background, pivoting towards a Scrum Master within Agile Digital Delivery in the most efficient way.

Among other things the book will teach you:

- What requirements apply to Scrum Master role candidates these days;

- How to deal with Recruiters and get your application through their initial filter;
- How different companies see Scrum Master roles and responsibilities;
- What are Agile Hybrid roles, and why should it concern Scrum Masters;
- How to do your research and other preparation properly;
- How to write a good to-the-point Cover Letter, and do you need one at all;
- How to reformat your Resume and present it the best possible way;
- What interview questions a new Scrum Master can expect, and the best ways to respond.

Sounds like something you or your colleagues could benefit from?

Well, then feel free to buy me another coffee and grab the book from Amazon today.

# About the Author

Dmitri Iarandine is a delivery-focused Transformation Leader and Coach, passionate about the New Ways of Working and Digital Disruption, helping companies define and implement the new operating models and optimization strategies that help them remain competitive and Customer-focused in the modern rapidly changing business landscape.

Dmitri is a pragmatic and hands-on Lean-Agile practitioner who introduces all the necessary concepts and hybrid models with the required blend of the elements that set foundation for a longer-term digital transformation, enabling faster feedback loops, empirical planning, reduction of risk, and more sustainable pace of value delivery to the Customer.

Professional Agile Coach and Trainer with 20 years of experience working in Software Development, Professional Services and Digital Delivery across multiple industries, Dmitri values and promotes collaboration and transparency on all levels, helping build bridges between the Business stakeholders and the IT.

Founder of **JoinAgile.com Initiative** helping the recruiters find the right Lean-Agile talent, using a new advanced professional competency testing system.